COLLEGE FINANCIAL AID

HOW TO

GET YOUR

FAIR SHARE

Peter V. Laurenzo, CFP

College Financial Aid: How To Get Your Fair Share

Copyright © 1991, 1993 by Peter V. Laurenzo.

Hudson Financial Press
74 Chapel Street, P.O. Box 1265
Albany, New York, 12201-1265

Cataloging-in-Publication Data
Laurenzo, Peter V.
College Financial Aid: How To Get Your Fair Share/
Peter V. Laurenzo

2nd Edition

ISBN 0-9629961-1-4

378.30973 – dc20

1. Student aid – United States –
   Handbooks, manuals, etc.
2. Scholarships
3. Student loan funds

NOTICE: This book is intended to provide useful and accurate information concerning college financial aid. Be aware that statutes and procedures are constantly evolving and can be subject to interpretation. It is the reader's responsibility to verify the information contained herein before relying on it. Neither the author nor the publisher makes any warranties concerning the information in this book.

This book is dedicated to the thousands
of families who paid more for their
college education than they
should have because they were either
misinformed or uninformed.

ABOUT THE AUTHOR

Peter V. Laurenzo is President of College Aid Planning Associates, Inc. based in Albany, N.Y. He holds a Masters degree in Education, is a Certified Financial Planner, and is a member of the International Association for Financial Planning, National Association of Student Financial Aid Administrators, and The American Council on Education. In addition to maintaining his full-time financial planning practice, Mr. Laurenzo presents financial aid seminars to employers and schools throughout New York State, holds national financial aid training workshops for other financial planners, and is a frequent guest on radio and television.

TABLE OF CONTENTS

INTRODUCTION

A few years ago, as a practicing financial planner, I became increasingly frustrated with the lack of information readily available to me and my clients regarding college financial aid. I began researching financial aid, analyzing the Federal financial aid formula and the effect the family's finances had on their aid eligibility. I became quite intrigued by the mysterious cloud cast over this subject. It seemed wherever I looked for information, the only pieces of the puzzle I found were ones I already had. It was evident that shedding light on this financial arena would be an answer to the needs of many parents and students. The demand for this information was profound, so, in addition to my regular practice, I began advising families on financial aid. Time after time, by utilizing sound financial planning principles, I am able to help families qualify for more financial aid than they would have received had they gone through the process alone. Knowledge and proper planning are the key ingredients to maximizing aid eligibility. Today, my college financial aid planning practice is virtually a full-time enterprise.

It is evident that families lose thousands of dollars of financial aid each year because they are uninformed or misinformed about how to plan for it. Many families who didn't qualify for any aid would have received aid with proper planning. Do all families qualify for financial aid? Of course not. There are many factors that determine how much a family is entitled to receive. But don't assume you're ineligible without first investigating the facts!

I am often asked if there are many families who don't have enough savings to pay for their child's education. I can safely say that 95% of my clients do not have adequate funds accumulated to send their children through four years of college. I unequivocally profess that savings should commence at an early age. You probably have seen charts and statistics illustrating how much you should be saving on a monthly basis to accumulate the amount of money you will need by the time your children reach college age. The reality is that most people will not accomplish this goal. It isn't because they weren't conscientious or didn't know how to plan. Unfortunately, during the eighteen years of raising children and preparing them for college, most families have not generated the cash flow or disposable income necessary to accumulate such an exorbitant amount of savings. If you feel you may have failed your children by not accumulating the dollars to fund their education, you are not alone — if misery loves company, join the crowd.

What I am going to present to you are sound financial aid planning principles to help you strategically plan for receiving your fair share of college financial aid. By utilizing this concise and non-technical format, parents and students will be able to understand, conceptualize and be pro-active through this often very confusing process.

This book will be an asset to families with students in college, students on the threshold of college and for families with young children who want to effectively plan for college. This information is critical whether you have no savings and need to know where the money will come from, or if you have accumulated savings and want to stretch it out as far as possible. Finally, this information should be coordinated with your investment advisor. Your financial objectives may be severely compromised if strategic planning for financial aid is not incorporated into a college savings program.

NOTICE: Unless specifically indicated, the information in this text is focused on dependent students. Although there is a commonality of financial aid principles with dependent and independent status, percentages, assessments and regulations may differ.

"Only families with pet dragons are eligible for financial aid."

FACT OR FICTION

Myth **There is little financial aid available.**

On the contrary, the Federal government alone has committed over $20 billion towards the cost of higher education for the 1993-94 school year. This, in addition to State aid programs and individual college aid programs, constitutes an enormous resource, if you know how to pursue it.

Myth **You have to be poor to receive financial aid.**

There are many families with incomes between $50,000 and $100,000 receiving financial aid.

Myth **There is no way to plan to maximize the amount of aid you may be eligible for.**

College financial aid is not a black and white process. This book will demonstrate how to effectively prepare yourself for financial aid. The employment of some basic planning techniques can result in an increase in financial aid from a few hundred to thousands of dollars each year.

Myth **The way to find money is to search for scholarships.**

Unfortunately too much effort is often dedicated to this pursuit. The vast majority of financial assistance will come from need-based financial aid. For more information on this "myth", read the section on Scholarship Search Services.

Myth **If your son or daughter moves or is ejected out of the house, they will be able to file as an independent.**

It's not quite that easy! There is specific criteria for establishing independent status. Carefully read the section on Dependent Versus Independent.

Myth **If I don't qualify for student aid, I'll take out Student Loans.**

Most student loans are need-based and have specific borrowing limits.

GETTING ACQUAINTED WITH THE SYSTEM

An Overview of Financial Aid

In order for the Federal government, as well as the colleges, to determine eligibility for financial aid, a financial aid form must be completed. All students applying for financial aid must complete the Free Application For Federal Student Aid (FAFSA). This application (instituted in 1993) qualifies students for Federal student aid programs. In addition to the FAFSA, many colleges and universities also require a Financial Aid Form (FAF). This additional information further qualifies the student for institutional aid, as well as giving the financial aid officer room to make professional judgement decisions regarding the student's need. Most financial aid forms are processed by either College Scholarship Services (CSS) in Princeton, New Jersey or by American College Testing Program (ACT) in Iowa City, Iowa. The Pennsylvania Higher Education Assistance Agency (PHEAA) and the ED Application Processor are also contracted for application processing. The information on the FAFSA is entered into the Federal

Needs Analysis Methodology which is used to calculate the student's Expected Family Contribution (EFC) for Federal aid. The Expected Family Contribution is how much the family will be responsible to pay for college before Federal aid eligibility commences. The EFC (often in conjunction with the FAF) is also used as a benchmark by many schools for determining how much institutional aid you may be eligible for.

The financial aid forms require information concerning student income and assets, parental income and assets, number of family members attending school, family size, and many other questions which are weighted in determining your Expected Family Contribution. Many applicants find the form intimidating and confusing. If you do, get help. It is frightening to recall the number of people who did not complete the form(s) because of their frustration with it. If you do not submit an aid form, you will get no aid.

After completing the financial aid form, it is mailed to the appropriate needs analysis processing center. The processing center enters the information into the Federal Needs Analysis Methodology, and an Expected Family Contribution Level is established. A Student Aid Report (SAR) is sent back to the student and a facsimile of that report to each of the colleges listed on the financial aid form.

Upon acceptance to each respective school, the Financial Aid Department will send the student an Award Letter. This is an itemized list of the kind(s) and amount(s) of financial aid that is being offered to the student. If the aid package is acceptable, it is signed and returned to the college. With the exception of completing loan applications, this concludes the process for that academic year. Each year, the process starts over with new forms and potentially new aid packages.

*"And I have orthodontic bills, and my property
taxes increased and..."*

COLLEGE COST

MINUS

EXPECTED FAMILY CONTRIBUTION

EQUALS

DEMONSTRATED FINANCIAL NEED

Expected Family Contribution

A critical component of the financial aid equation is the student's Expected Family Contribution (EFC). The EFC is the sum of the parents' contribution and the student's contribution. The EFC, minus the total cost of the school, is the amount of need you are demonstrating, and therefore the amount of aid you are eligible for. For financial aid purposes, a budget (total cost of the school) is established by each individual school. The budgeted costs will include tuition, room and board, miscellaneous fees, personal expenses, and a travel allowance. If the cost of the school is more than the EFC, you have demonstrated need. If the cost of the school is less than the EFC, you are not demonstrating need and are therefore ineligible for need-based financial aid.

A student applies to a school with a total cost of $16,000 and has a $9,000 Expected Family Contribution Level. That student has demonstrated $7,000 of need, and therefore can be eligible for $7,000 of aid. That student also applies to a school costing $8,000. Since the Expected Family Contribution Level is $9,000, need has not been demonstrated.

Aid Comes From

Federal →
→
→
GRANTS
LOANS
WORK STUDY

State → GRANTS

College →
→
GRANTS

COLLEGE JOB
SERVICE

Where Financial Aid Comes From

Financial aid flows from three primary sources:

Federal Aid: The Federal Government disseminates aid in the form of grants, loans and work-study programs.

State Aid: All states have aid programs which the student may be eligible for. They may include grants and loans as well as special subsidies. (Since all state aid programs vary, you should check with the appropriate agency in the state you reside). Generally, state aid is not available for nonresidents.

Institutional Aid: Grants and need-based scholarships constitute the majority of institutional (college) aid.

The maximum amount of Federal and State aid available will often be insufficient to offset demonstrated need. It is the decision of the college to determine how much of that deficit will be made up by their own funds. Some schools will meet that deficit totally, thus the percent of need met would be 100%. Some schools will offer no grant aid while some schools will offer partial grant aid. It is no secret that some schools are reaping larger endowments and grants than others; thus more funds can be allocated to students in need.

It is important to remember that the financial aid process, like filing income taxes, occurs every year. If there are dramatic changes in a family's financial or personal situation in any given year, it is likely that the subsequent aid packages will reflect those changes.

Students are notified of the type of aid package the school is offering in the form of an award letter. The award letter breaks down the aid for the following school year. The composition or makeup of the aid being offered should be scrutinized. Financial aid can be classified into two categories: self-help and gift aid. Self-help includes loans and work study programs while gift aid is composed of grants and scholarships. You may have two like-priced schools and be offered the same dollar amount of aid, but have compositions which are totally different. One school may be heavily weighted in the self-help area, whereas the other school may offer more gift aid. Obviously, the latter is a more desirous package, since gift aid does not have to be repaid. By applying to more than one school, you will have the opportunity to "shop" the financial aid packages.

I recently met with a client whose expected family contribution was $10,000 and had applied to two schools with identical costs. Both schools offered an aid package of $8,000 (the difference between their contribution level and the college's budgeted cost of $18,000). School A offered a $2,500 Stafford Loan, $1,500 of Work-Study and and a $4,000 institutional grant. School B's package was comprised of a $2,000 Stafford Loan, and a $6,000 institutional grant. Although both schools met 100% of the demonstrated need, School B offered a better aid package.

Recapping the Process

☐ The financial aid form is completed by the student and/or parents.

☐ The form is sent to a needs analysis processing center.

☐ Four to six weeks after the form is sent, a Student Aid Report (SAR) is generated and mailed back to the family and a facsimile of that report is sent to the schools listed on the financial aid form.

After the student has been accepted at a school, the school sends an award letter to the student, notifying him/her of the aid package for the subsequent school year.

AID SEQUENCE

FINANCIAL AID FORM

NEEDS ANALYSIS CENTER

STUDENT AID REPORT

AWARD LETTER

Don't Assume Ineligibility!

I can not overemphasize the importance of completing a financial aid form.

Recently, I met with clients with two children in college. Jason (a sophomore) is attending a school with a price tag of $20,000, while Jennifer (a junior) is enrolled in a $16,000 college. Until they met with me, they had never completed a financial aid form. They initially believed they were ineligible for aid (with combined incomes of nearly $60,000), and after scrutinizing the financial aid form, decided not to complete it. Upon looking at their income and assets, and inputting the necessary information into an in-house Federally-approved needs analysis program, we arrived at an estimated Family Contribution Level of $7,500 per child. This means that if they had completed the aid form, Jason would have been eligible for $12,500 of aid, while Jennifer would have been eligible for $8,500. $21,000 errors happen too frequently.

"Student assets – that'll be 35% please."

Financial Aid Planning Strategies

Student Assets

The impact of student assets in the Federal formula is simple and profound. Whether the student has $100 or $10,000 dollars, 35% of the value is assessed and added to the student's contribution. For example, $5,000 has been saved in the student's name and that amount in entered on the financial aid form under student assets. The family contribution level will increase by $1,750 ($5,000 x 35%). Financial planners, investment advisers, insurance agents and tax accountants generally advise their clients to save money in their children's name to take advantage of lower marginal tax brackets. The impact of this is about 13% less taxes paid on *interest or dividends earned.* If the student is eligible for aid, the impact is *35% of the whole investment.* The bottom line is, if there is a breath of a chance of receiving financial aid, don't save in the student's name.

So where should you save? If the student has a younger sibling (the younger the better) save the money in his or her name. It won't be assessed as student or parental assets. (I do not advocate having children every five years to shelter assets.) If this isn't possible, you are better off saving in the parent's name since the maximum assessment is only about 6% (rather than 35%). This is a serious inequity within the Federal formula. Mr. Wood saves $10,000 in his daughter's name and has $3,500 of student assets added to their family contribution level. Mr. Smart saves $10,000 in his own name and has $600 of assets added to their family contribution level. Both families made the same sacrifices to help fund their child's education but because Mr. Wood was *uninformed,* it potentially will cost him $2,900 more than Mr. Smart! Why don't the colleges tell you this?

Many clients already have savings programs established for their children and ask what to do with them. First of all, it is legal to gift up to $10,000 per person each year without creating a gift tax problem. If the savings can be legally moved, then move them. I often recommend that students with minimal savings use that money on college supplies that will have to be purchased anyway, rather than list them on the form. Assets and corresponding debts are valued on the financial aid form at *time of application.* If there is a large sum of money in the student's name that cannot be legally moved, then spend it first towards college costs. If you don't, the remaining balance will be *reassessed at 35%* when you complete your next financial aid form.

This brings to mind a case where a financial planner recommended a college savings program (for a 10 year old) utilizing zero coupon bonds maturing at the beginning of each year of college. The value of each bond at maturity was $4,000. Although the intentions of the planner were admirable, he was not aware of the financial aid implications of his recommendations. The following demonstrates the impact of this plan:

Value of bonds		Assessment		Aid Reductions
Year 1: $4,000	X	35%	=	$1,400
3,600	X	35%	=	1,260
3,200	X	35%	=	1,120
2,800	X	35%	=	980
				4,760
Year 2: 4,000	X	35%	=	1,400
3,600	X	35%	=	1,260
2,800	X	35%	=	1,120
				3,780
Year 3: 4,000	X	35%	=	1,400
3,600	X	35%	=	1,260
				2,660
Year 4: 4,000	X	35%	=	1,400
				$12,600
				Total Aid Reductions

Summary:	$16,000	Worth of bonds
	- 12,600	Financial aid reductions
	$ 3,400	Net

What the Planner should have done was to recommend bonds that matured when the prospective student completed the sophomore year in high school, then shift the assets out of the student's name, or, kept the bonds in either a younger sibling's or parent's name.

Parental Assets

As previously stated, the maximum assessment on parental assets is approximately 6% in the Federal Formula. Let's define what assets they're talking about. You must include all cash savings (cash, checking account balances, passbook savings, certificates of deposit, money market accounts, etc.). They also want to know the value of your stocks, bonds, mutual funds, and other securities, real estate you own, as well as the net value of a business or farm that you have ownership in. A significant change resulting from the "Higher Education Amendments of 1992" is the equity in your personal residence, as well as a family farm upon which the family resides, is no longer an assessable asset for *Federal* financial aid. However, most colleges and universities that offer institutional aid *are not excluding your home or farm from assessments* when determining institutional aid eligibility.

You do not list consumer assets such as automobiles, furnishings, recreational vehicles, etc.

Unlike student assets, the Formula does not assess parental assets from the first dollar. An Asset Protection Allowance (see pgs 18 & 19) protects some of your net worth from being considered available for college expenses. The age of the oldest parent is a question on the financial aid form. As the age of the parent increases, the allowance increases. This may be one of the few times in your life when being older is a benefit. For example, if there are two parents in the household, and the oldest parent is 45, the Asset Protection Allowance is $36,600. If the total value of your assets is $60,000, only $23,400 ($60,000 - $36,600) would be assessed. If there was only one parent in the household and that parent was 45, the allowance would be $26,300. The Asset Protection

Allowance range for two parents is from $2,200 at age 26, to $66,800 (if the oldest parent is 65 or older).

Assets that are excluded for Federal purposes are pension funds, IRA's, TSA's, Keoghs, 401k's, annuities, and the value of life insurance policies. Elective contributions to some of these plans will be carried back as untaxed income on the form, but the value of these assets remains sheltered.

ASSET PROTECTION ALLOWANCE

(TWO PARENTS – DEPENDENT STUDENT)

TOTAL NET VALUE OF ASSETS	**$50,000**
ASSET PROTECTION ALLOWANCE (OLDEST PARENT AGE 45)	**$34,200**
AMOUNT OF PARENTAL ASSETS ASSESSED FOR FAMILY CONTRIBUTION	**$15,800**

ASSET ALLOWANCE TABLES

DEPENDENT STUDENTS

IF THE AGE OF THE OLDER PARENT IS:	THEN THE ASSET PROTECTION ALLOWANCE IS:	
	TWO PARENTS	ONE PARENT
25 or less	0	0
26	2,200	1,600
27	4,300	3,200
28	6,500	4,700
29	8,600	6,300
30	10,800	7,900
31	13,000	9,500
32	15,100	11,100
33	17,300	12,600
34	19,400	14,200
35	21,600	15,800
36	23,800	17,400
37	25,900	19,000
38	28,100	20,500
39	30,200	22,100
40	32,500	23,700
41	33,300	24,100
42	34,100	24,700
43	35,000	25,200
44	35,700	25,800
45	36,600	26,300
46	37,600	26,900
47	38,800	27,600
48	39,800	28,200
49	40,800	28,800
50	41,800	29,500
51	43,200	30,200
52	44,300	31,100
53	45,700	31,800
54	47,100	32,600
55	48,300	33,400
56	49,800	34,400
57	51,300	35,200
58	52,900	36,200
59	54,800	37,200
60	56,500	38,100
61	58,500	39,200
62	60,300	40,300
63	62,400	41,500
64	64,600	42,800
65 or more	66,800	44,000

ASSET ALLOWANCE TABLES
INDEPENDENT STUDENTS

IF THE AGE OF THE STUDENT IS:	THEN THE ASSET PROTECTION ALLOWANCE IS:	
	MARRIED	UNMARRIED
25 or less	0	0
26	2,200	1,600
27	4,300	3,200
28	6,500	4,700
29	8,600	6,300
30	10,800	7,900
31	13,000	9,500
32	15,100	11,100
33	17,300	12,600
34	19,400	14,200
35	21,600	15,800
36	23,800	17,400
37	25,900	19,000
38	28,100	20,500
39	30,200	22,100
40	32,400	23,700
41	33,300	24,100
42	34,100	24,700
43	35,000	25,200
44	35,700	25,800
45	36,600	26,300
46	37,600	26,900
47	38,800	27,600
49	40,800	28,800
50	41,800	29,500
51	43,200	30,200
52	44,300	31,100
53	45,700	31,800
54	47,100	32,600
55	48,300	33,400
56	49,800	34,400
57	51,300	35,200
58	52,900	36,200
59	54,800	37,200
60	56,500	38,100
61	58,500	39,200
62	60,300	40,300
63	62,400	41,500
64	64,600	42,800
65 or more	66,800	44,000

"Assets? ...What Assets?"

Sheltering Assets

Often parents want to shelter some of their savings for other purposes, such as retirement. My first recommendation is investing in fixed annuities. These tax-deferred investments are not assessed for Federal aid and can often be purchased without any sales or administrative charges. The only drawback is they follow the 59-½ rules. Monies taken out prior to age 59-½ are subject to a 10% tax penalty, as well as being taxed as ordinary income. This isn't necessarily the end of the world. If after-tax money was invested (which is usually the case), the penalty and taxes would only be on the interest earned. If you were in an aid position, you probably would have lost 6% a year on the total investment (if it was not sheltered). Life insurance is another option for sheltering assets. Buy life insurance only if you have an insurance need. Insurance policies have considerable charges built into their contracts because they are insuring you. These charges will obviously impact your rate of return.

Valuation of Assets

Since assets are heavily weighted in the Formula, it is important that they are valued correctly. For most families, their most valuable asset is their home. You are asked how much your home is worth. Do not use assessed value, insured value or tax value. Your home is worth what someone will pay for it in a reasonable period of time. This is not the time to admire the deck you built last summer and believe it has increased your home value tenfold. For the last few years, home values have showed little appreciation in most areas of the

United States. A home selling for $125,000 in 1988 may only yield $100,000 today. Use a conservative but realistic home value.

Families have erroneously stated the amount of savings bonds at their face value. Remember, it takes years for these bonds to mature and they may currently be worth only a fraction of their face value. If you are unsure, check with your local bank. If you own stocks or mutual funds, check their current price the day you complete your form.

Placing a value on a business or rental property should be determined by estimating its fair market value. The business value includes the value of land, buildings, machinery, equipment, inventories, etc., on the day the financial aid form is signed. How much do you think someone would pay you for your business or business property? Be sure to list any debts against the business. It is the net value that is assessed in the needs analysis formula.

Trust Funds

Trust funds in the name of a specific individual should be reported as that person's assets on the application. In the case of divorce or separation where the trust is owned jointly, and ownership is not being contested, the property and the debt is equally divided between the owners for reporting purposes, unless the terms of the trust specify some other method of division.

As a general rule, the value of the trust must be reported as an asset, even if the beneficiary's access to the trust is restricted. If the grantor of a trust has voluntarily placed restrictions on the use of the trust, then the trust would be reported in the same manner as a trust that did not have any specific restrictions. The way in which the trust must be reported varies according to whether the student (or dependent student's parent) receives or will receive the interest income of the principal of the trust, or both.

Interest only. If a student, spouse, or parent receives only the interest from the trust, any interest received in the base year must be reported as income. Even if the interest accumulates in the trust and is not paid out during the year, the person who will receive the interest must report an asset value for the interest he or she will receive in the future. The present value of the interest the person will receive while the trust exists can usually be calculated by the trust officer. This value represents the amount a third person would be willing to pay in order to receive the interest income that the student (or parent) will receive from the trust in the future.

Principal only. The student, spouse, or parents who will receive only the trust principal must report the present value of his or her right to the trust principal as an asset. For example, if the principal is $10,000 and reverts to a dependent student's parents when the trust ends in 10 years, but the student is receiving the interest earned from the trust, the present value of the parents' right to the principal of the trust must be reported as a parental asset. The present value of the principal is the amount that a third person would pay at the present time for the right to receive the principal 10 years from now (basically, the amount that one would have to deposit now to receive $10,000 in 10 years, including the accumulated interest). Again, the present value can be calculated by the trust officer.

Both Principal and Interest. If a student, spouse, or parent receives both the interest and principal from the trust, the present value of both interest and principal would be reported, as described above. If the trust is set up in such a manner that the interest accumulates within the trust until the trust ends, the beneficiary should report as an asset the present value of the funds (both interest and principal) that he or she is expected to receive when the trust ends.

If a trust has been restricted by court order, it would not be reported as an asset. One example of such a restricted trust is one that was set up by court order to pay for future surgery for the victim of a car accident.

Debt

The Formula does take debt into consideration when assessing your assets. Mortgages, home equity loans, and investment debt will offset your assets. Assets minus liabilities equal net worth. If your home is valued at $100,000 and you have a $60,000 mortgage, your net equity is $40,000. The treatment of the equity in your home is no different from money in the bank. As previously mentioned, home equity *is not* assessed for Federal aid purposes anymore, but is often assessed by schools in determining their own aid eligibility. Consumer debts, however, are not considered liabilities for financial aid purposes. It often makes a lot of sense to consolidate auto loans, charge card loans, etc. into a home equity loan prior to filing for financial aid. Not only do you increase the potential for more aid eligibility, but you will be paying interest that in most cases is tax deductible.

In 1989, I was a guest on a local radio show. A woman called and explained that she thought that the poorer you were, the more aid you would receive. She proceeded to tell me that she had "maxed" out her credit cards and bought an expensive car, thus creating a large auto loan. She was quite surprised to hear that her amassed debt would have no impact on Federal aid. The moral of the story is — stay out of consumer debt.

MORTGAGES
AND
HOME EQUITY LOANS
REDUCE
PARENTAL NET ASSETS
FOR INSTITUTIONAL AID

STAY OUT OF CONSUMER DEBT!

"Is this what you call getting hit with both barrels?"

Student Income

Both parental income and student income are based on earnings received during the calendar year preceding the school year which aid is being applied for. If there is one area in the Formula which is ludicrous, it is the assessment on student income. Fifty percent of after-tax income (reduced from 70% in 1992) is added to the student contribution. A positive change enacted in 1992 is a $1,750 income protection allowance for a dependent student. The 50% assessment is on earnings that exceed $1,750. What a disincentive to earn more than $1,750. For example, in January of Sandra's senior year in high school, she begins working a part-time job and earns $4,000 by the end of the summer. When she completes her financial aid form for her *sophomore* year, approximately $1,000 will be added to her contribution level. (Note: the amount is adjusted due to FICA and taxes.) This assessment not only includes earned income, but it also includes unearned income (interest and dividends). Recall the example of the student who had saved $10,000 in his name and was assessed 35% of the asset. If he had earned 8% on that $10,000 or $800.00, approximately 50% of that interest income would have been added to the student contribution!

It is important to note that earnings from Federal Work Study programs that are based on need are excluded from student income. These earnings are taxable, but should be subtracted from the student's adjusted gross income when completing the financial aid forms.

Parental Income

The best piece of advice I can give regarding parental income is: Don't quit your day job. After certain income allowances, the assessment on parent income increases from 22% to 47%. The rate is based on the principle that as income increases beyond the amount needed to maintain a basic standard of living, the portion used for family maintenance decreases, while the portion available for discretionary purposes increases. Since the highest offset is less than 50%, you will be better off with an aid reduction than not earning that extra dollar. It is important to note that adjusted gross income is a key factor in the formula. Business or rental losses that flow to page one of your IRS Form 1040 are helpful.

As with student income, unearned income (interest, dividends, capital gains, etc.) is treated the same as earned income. The money growing tax-deferred in your IRA or 401K, etc., will not be counted, but you must include your elective contributions to these plans as untaxed income on the financial aid form. Tax-free income and untaxed social security benefits are also assessed and must be included on the financial aid form. Remember, the tax-deferred asset is not included on the form, but the pre-tax contribution to that asset is carried back as untaxed income.

For example, each year Mr. Smith electively contributes $2,600 (pretax) to his 401K plan at work. His balance in the plan is currently $30,000. Mr. Smith must list $2,600 as untaxed income on the financial aid form, but does not have to show his $30,000 balance.

How Parental Income Is Factored

TAXABLE INCOME:

Wages, Salaries, Tips
Interest Income
Dividend Income
Net Income (or Loss) from a business, farm, rents, etc.
Other Taxable Income (alimony, capital gains, pensions, etc.)

NON-TAXABLE INCOME:

Deductible IRA and/or Keogh Payments
Earned Income Credits
Untaxed Portions of Pensions
Tax-Exempt Interest Income
Payments to Tax-Deferred Pension and Savings Plans
Social Security Benefits
Workmens Compensation
Disability Benefits
Child Support

= TOTAL INCOME

ALLOWANCES AGAINST PARENTS' INCOME:

U.S. Income Taxes Paid
State and Local Tax Allowance
Social Security Tax
Income Protection Allowance (based on family size)
Employment Expense Allowance

= TOTAL ALLOWANCES

> ### TOTAL INCOME
> ### − TOTAL ALLOWANCES
> ### = AVAILABLE INCOME

"Hail Alma Mater..."

Number of Family Members Attending School

As previously stated, the family contribution level is comprised of the parents' contribution and the student's contribution. The financial aid form asks how many family members will be attending college at least half time (including parents). The more family members attending, the lower your expected contribution level. Suppose the Jones have one child (Chris) going to college. After completing the financial aid form, their contribution level was $10,000, $9,200 from the parents and $800 from the student. Chris is going to a school with a comprehensive cost of $9,000. It doesn't appear there will be any Federal aid for Chris. Suddenly, Mom decides to go half-time at the local community college. The cost for each course is $250.00, so Mom will spend $1,000 for the year for four courses. This change will halve the parents contribution to $4,600 ($9,200 divided by 2) and change Chris's expected family contribution to $5,400 ($4,600 + $800). Now Chris is eligible for $3,600 of aid, and if this need is met, it's like paying Mom $2,600 ($3,600 - $1,000 tuition) to go to school. Mom must attend an accredited school half-time for at least one term, working towards a degree or certificate leading to a recognized education credential.

Although Mom's attendance will certainly increase Christopher's Federal aid eligibility, there is no warranty that the school is going to increase his aid with their own grant money. Although most schools financially recognize more than one sibling in school when formulating financial aid packages, many schools will add little or nothing to the package when the second student is a parent.

For the families who had their children close together, it proves to be quite advantageous. Actually, this part of the formula is very logical. If the government feels you can afford to pay a certain dollar amount for one student's education, then it makes sense that you can only afford to pay half of that amount with two in school, or a third of that amount with three in school. What often happens is that one student who is attending a low cost school still has little or no aid eligibility, but positively impacts the other student who is attending a more expensive school.

SPECIAL CONSIDERATIONS

Deadlines

Most schools will require that the financial aid form be completed and mailed to the appropriate processing center by a specific date. This date will be after January 1 of the same year preceding the fall semester. It is important to adhere to these deadlines to ensure that you don't lose the opportunity to receive any aid you could be eligible for. If the student is applying to schools with different aid deadlines, be certain to send your form out by the earliest required date.

A problem many families are faced with is the inability to complete their income tax forms by the aid deadline. Some schools will require the financial aid forms to be submitted as early as January 15. W-2 and 1099 forms usually haven't been received by this date, so it is impossible to complete your taxes. If you are faced with early deadlines, you will have to estimate your tax return and use the estimated figures on your financial aid form. You will then check the box on the form stating the income information is based on an estimated tax return. I strongly suggest to use information from a completed tax return whenever possible, however, do not miss deadlines because your taxes are not finished. When estimating taxes, use your last pay stub to determine income, check bankbooks to see how much interest was earned and approximate your itemized deductions. Since tax tables change every year, use current tables to determine your taxes paid. A common mistake in completing the line "taxes paid" is entering how much tax was withheld from your earnings. Taxes paid is your tax liability on net taxable income. This number is derived from the tax schedules.

A final note concerning deadlines. The sooner you can complete your aid form prior to the deadline, the better. The early bird may get the fattest worm.

"Does this mean I'm independent?"

Dependent Versus Independent

When a student is classified as independent, parental income and assets are not assessed in the Federal formula. Obviously, if parents have high income and assets, there is a strong advantage in not including them on the financial aid form. The misinformation for determining independence for financial aid purposes is abundant, and sometimes incredible. The most common question is, "If I don't claim my son or daughter on my tax return, or if I throw them out of the house, they will be emancipated, right?" Wrong! If it were that easy, we would all throw our kids out.

For Federal financial aid purposes, the student must meet one of following six conditions to be considered independent:

1. For the 1993-94 school year, you were born before 1/1/70.

2. You are a U.S. Armed Forces veteran

> **Definition** - A student who is a veteran of active service in the U.S. Army, Navy, Air Force, Marines or Coast Guard; or a student who is or was a National Guard or Reserves enlistee who participated in Operation Desert Shield/Storm and was discharged from active duty.

3. You are a ward of the courts or both parents are dead.

4. You have legal dependents (other than a spouse) and are providing at least half of their support.

5. You are married.

6. You are a graduate or professional student.

It should be noted that the criteria for establishing independence for Federal aid may be different than the criteria for establishing independence for state or institutional aid. Check with your State and college and ask what guidelines they have for independent status.

The financial aid administrator may override the student's dependency status in individual cases if he or she decides that the student should be considered independent.

Single Parents - Remarried Parents

Perhaps one of the most confusing elements of completing the financial aid form is when the natural parents are divorced. Dealing with this issue for Federal aid purposes is actually quite simple. The income and assets of the custodial parent must be entered on the financial aid form. The custodial parent is the parent with whom the student lived with the most during the last twelve months. If the custodial parent is remarried, the income and assets of the spouse are included. The amount of child support received from the non-custodial parent will also be entered on the form.

Separation of Parents. If a separation has occurred, the same rules as for a divorce should be used to determine which parent's information must be reported. The separation need not be a legal separation – the student's parents may consider themselves separated when one of the parents has left the household for an indefinite period of time, and no longer makes a substantial contribution to the finances of the household. However, if the parents still live in the same house, they would not be considered to be separated, and information for both parents must be reported.

There are cases where the student is living with a relative, but the relative has not been appointed a legal guardian. Although the student is receiving support from the relative, their financial information will not impact the student's aid eligibility. For example, John has lived with his grandparents for the past two years while attending high school. Although his grandparents have supported John, they are not treated as a parent of the student and their financial situation would have no bearing on John's aid eligibility.

A Legal Guardian *is* treated in the same manner as a natural parent, if he or she has been appointed by the court to support the student.

Foster parents *are not* treated as a parent of the student.

A stepparent's information is reported if the stepparent is married to the student's responsible natural parent or if the student has been legally adopted by the stepparent. If the natural parent has died and the stepparent survives, then the student is independent (assuming the student is not dependent on the surviving natural parent), unless the stepparent legally adopted the student.

Death of a Parent. If one, but not both, of the student's parents has died, the student would only answer the dependency questions for the surviving parent, and would not report any financial information for the deceased parent on the financial aid form. If both the student's parents are dead when the student fills out the financial aid form, the student will be independent.

In the event that a separation, divorce or death occurred in the year prior to applying for financial aid, and a joint income tax return is filed, only the income of the custodial or surviving parent is entered on the financial aid form. The custodial parent should only list his or her portion of assets and liabilities. For example, if the parent's home is valued at $100,000 with a mortgage balance of $60,000 (assuming 50% ownership), the custodial parent would list $50,000 for the value of the home and $30,000 as debt.

Special Situations

The Free Application For Federal Student Aid (FAFSA) no longer collects information on special circumstances. In the past there were questions regarding dislocated workers, high medical expenses etc. However, there is a statement in Section G that tells you to notify the financial aid administrator if you have "unusual circumstances not covered on this form that would affect your eligibility for student financial aid." This format is not very appealing, since it puts the responsibility on the student (or parents) to make the college aware of your circumstances. In addition, without 20-20 vision, you probably would miss these minuscule instructions.

If you have high medical and dental expenses, pay elementary or secondary private school tuition (for children other than the applicant), have lost your job, or been notified that you will be laid off, or have any other extraordinary financial or personal circumstances (death or divorce) that will impact your ability to pay college costs, you must notify the financial aid administrator at the school the student is or will be attending. The financial aid officer can use "professional judgement" on a case-by-case basis to adjust data items in the Formula.

Case One: A family with $6,000 of non-reimbursed medical expenses has an adjusted gross income of $30,000. The aid administrator might decide to adjust the reported AGI to take into account the unusually high expenses.

Case Two: A parent has been notified that he will be laid off in the imminent future. The aid administrator may decide to substitute expected income for the year rather than the previous earned income.

Since professional judgement involves a certain degree of subjectivity, students applying to a number of schools should make all aid administrators aware of their circumstances. You will find that some schools will be more flexible than others.

"Maybe I should go to college to learn how to do these forms."

THE PROCESS

Completing the Federal Financial Aid Form

To be considered for virtually any type of financial aid, a financial aid form must be filled out and sent to a centralized processing center. Most people find financial aid forms confusing, so don't feel too inadequate if you are experiencing difficulty completing the form. It is extremely important to complete these forms correctly and have them sent in on time. Financial aid forms that are rejected and sent back to the applicant may ultimately miss deadlines and thus jeopardize aid.

If there is a professional agency in your area that specializes in form completion, it may be well worth your while to employ them. Some college financial aid offices may offer help with the form (particularly if the student is applying to that school). Your tax preparer will understand the income elements that need to be completed, but don't expect them to have a vast background with the intricacies of financial aid. Remember, the foundation for aid will be based on the information submitted.

For the 1993-94 school year, a new Free Application For Federal Student Aid (FAFSA) was introduced.

All students applying for Federal financial aid must complete this form. What has been confusing during this application year is that many colleges and universities, in addition to the FAFSA, have also required a Financial Aid Form (FAF) be completed. To determine whether the FAF is necessary, look in the FAF instruction booklet to find the code listing for the school the student is applying to. If the school is listed, the FAF is required. If there is an asterisk next to the code number, the FAF is optional. If the school is not listed, only the FAFSA is required. (If the student is applying to multiple schools and only some schools have code numbers, the student should list only those schools with code numbers on the FAF, but list *all* schools on the FAFSA.) The reason many colleges want the FAF (in addition to the FAFSA) is to further qualify the student for aid eligibility. For example, beginning in 1993-94, the equity in your home is not a factor for determining Federal aid eligibility, thus it does not appear on the FAFSA. At many schools, however, they are continuing to weigh the equity in your home. Home equity questions do appear on the FAF.

Completing The FAFSA

Section A: Yourself

The student must give a home mailing address (rather than a school or office address). The student's state of legal residence identifies the agency to which information will be sent if the student has authorized such a release in Section G of the form. For a dependent student, the state of legal residence is usually the state in which the parents reside.

If the student fills out a FAFSA and omits his or her social security number, it will not be processed.

A student's marital status affects the treatment of his or her income and assets in the Federal formula. Marital status cannot be projected— the student must report marital status on the date of the application.

The FAFSA asks if the student will have his or her bachelor's degree before July 1 preceding the school year he or she is applying for aid. If the student answers "yes" to this question, there will be no eligibility for the Federal Pell Grant and FSEOG programs.

Section B: Student Status

A student is automatically considered independent if he or she meets at least one of the criteria previously mentioned. (See "Dependent versus Independent.") A student meeting one of these criteria is considered independent even if the student is still living with his or her parents.

Section C: Household Information

The following individuals may be included in the household size of the dependent student:

1. The student.

2. The student's parent(s), excluding a parent not living in the household as a result of death, separation or divorce.

3. The student's siblings, if they received or will receive more than half of their support from the student's parent(s) for the following academic year.

4. The student's children, if they receive or will receive more than half of their support from the student's parent(s) for the following academic year.

5. The student's parent's unborn child and/or the student's unborn child, if that child will be born before or during the award year and the student's parents will provide at least half the support.

6. Other persons, if they live with and receive more than one half of their support from the parent's at the time of application and will continue to receive that support for the award year.

Number in College

The number in college includes all those in household size who are attending a postsecondary educational institution at least half-time. To be considered for this purpose, the institution must be licensed by its state agency or be accredited by a nationally recognized accrediting agency.

Section D: Income, Earnings, and Benefits

Foreign Income

Income earned in a foreign country is treated in the same way as income earned in the United States. The value of foreign income (and taxes paid, if any) should be reported in U.S. dollars (using the exchange rate at the time of application).

Income Earned From Work

Parent(s) should list their individual earned income. This information is used to provide an offset for two working parents (enacted in 1992).

Untaxed Income and Benefits

Under "untaxed income and benefits", separate line items are provided for Social Security benefits, AFDC payments, and child support because these are the most common forms of untaxed income and benefits. Note that if Social Security benefits are paid to the parents on behalf of the student (because the student was under 18 years old at the time), those benefits are *reported as the parent's income,* not the student's income. Be certain not to include any portion of Social Security income that was taxable.

Earned income credits, as well as tax exempt interest, must be included as untaxed income.

Any voluntary pretax contribution to an IRA, Keogh, 401K, 403B (tax-deferred annuity) which results in a reduction in your taxable income will be included as untaxed income.

Housing allowances provided to the parents or student must be reported under "untaxed income and benefits." This applies to compensation that some people, particularly clergy and military personnel, receive for their jobs.

Excluded forms of income

Student financial assistance. With the exception of veterans educational and compensatory benefits, student financial assistance is not reported on the application.

Work-study earnings. If earnings are part of a financial aid package and are intended as financial assistance to the student, they are not reported as income.

Subsidized housing. Rent subsidies paid by government and charitable organizations for low-income housing are not reported as untaxed income.

Forced sale proceeds. Income received from the sale of farm or business assets should not be reported if the sale results from a voluntary or involuntary foreclosure, forfeiture, bankruptcy, or an involuntary liquidation.

Food Stamps, heating/fuel assistance, and child care benefits are not counted as income.

Section E:
Federal Stafford Loan Information

Information about Federal Stafford Loans, Federal Insured Student Loans (FISL), or any part of a Consolidation Loan used to repay Stafford Loans or FISLs should be included in this section. Don't include Federal Supplemental Loans for Students (SLS), Federal Plus Loans to students or parents, or Federal Perkins Loans. If the student has attended more than one college, he or she should include all Stafford Loans received at each college. If the student received more than one loan during the school year, he or she should be sure to include the total amount borrowed for that year. If the student has made any payments, he or she should subtract the total principal repaid from the amount borrowed.

Section F:
Veterans Educational Benefits

The applicant must report the amount of monthly benefits that he or she expects to receive during the award year. Included in this section are benefits from Selective Reserve Pay, New GI Bill, Vocational Rehabilitation, REPS, Educational Assistance Program, and Dependents Educational Assistance Program.

Section G:
College Release and Certification

This section permits the student to list six colleges that he or she may attend. Students can send information to additional schools by correcting school names on the Student Aid Report (SAR). This is addressed on Page 54.

Although parental information must be provided for a dependent student, a third party (such as another relative, a counselor, or a financial aid administrator) may sign the application in place of the parent(s) if:

the parent(s) is not currently in the United States

the current address of the parent is not known; or

the parent(s) has been determined physically or mentally incapable of providing a signature.

Preparer's Use Only

The law requires that if anyone other than the student, the student's spouse, or the student's parents prepared the application, the preparer must complete this section. Preparers must complete this section even if they are not paid for their services.

Section H: Asset Information

An asset is property owned by the family that has an exchange value. Possessions such as a car, a stereo, clothes or furniture are not reported as assets on the financial aid form.

Part ownership of an asset.

If the parent or student only has part ownership of the asset, that part should be reported.

Contested ownership.

Assets should not be reported if the ownership is being contested. For instance, if the parents are separated and they may not sell or borrow against jointly owned property that is being contested, the responsible parent would not list any value for the property or debts against it. However, if the ownership of the property is not being contested, the property would be reported as an asset.

Other Real Estate and Investment Value

"Investments" include a wide range of investments, including trust funds, money market funds, certificates of deposit, stocks, bonds, other securities, installment and land sale contracts, commodities, and precious and strategic metals. Investments also include money loaned out by the student or parent. Real estate includes second or summer homes or rental properties. The value of real estate and investments is the market value at the time the application was signed and dated.

Business.

Report the current market value of a business including land, buildings, machinery, equipment, inventories, etc. Don't include the home, even if it is part of the business. Then write in what is owed on the business, including the unpaid mortgage and related debts.

Farm.

When reporting the current market value of a farm, the student should include the value of the land, buildings, machinery, equipment, livestock, and inventories. The amount of farm debt reported should include the unpaid mortgage and related debts, as well as any loan for which the farm assets were used as collateral.

Section I: State Information

Students who are applying for state aid in Arkansas, California, Florida, Indiana, Iowa, Maryland, Massachusetts, Maine, Michigan, Minnesota, New Jersey, New York, North Dakota, Ohio, Pennsylvania, Rhode Island, Vermont, Washington, or West Virginia must fill out this section. These states and some others may require that the student answer additional questions.

The College Financial Aid Form

In addition to the Federal financial aid forms, some colleges will also have you complete their own aid form. This is sent directly back to the college and not to a processing center. Fortunately, the colleges' aid forms are usually much shorter and easier to complete. Each school may set its own criteria for institutional aid, thus questions may be asked concerning the family's finances which are not asked on the Federal form. I find it disconcerting that some colleges request information such as the value of IRA accounts, pension plans, the amount of life insurance on the parents, etc. This information doesn't necessarily have to impact your aid package, but it does raise the question of why they ask for this information. Unfortunately, if you don't complete their aid forms, you may not be considered for any institutional aid.

A common question on college forms is how much the family is willing to contribute towards the student's education. In my opinion, this is one of those no-win (or lose-lose) questions. If you indicate a dollar amount that is higher than what the school determines to be your expected contribution, it would be unlikely that they would give you more than you stated you could pay. If you grossly underestimate what the school determines to be your expected contribution, they will more than likely ignore your figures. I personally would rather be ignored than take the chance of losing aid. Be conservative if this question is asked.

The Student Aid Report (SAR)

Four to six weeks after sending the financial aid form to the appropriate processing center, the student will receive a Student Aid Report (SAR). The instructions state, based on the information submitted, whether you are eligible for a Federal Pell Grant. Don't be discouraged if you're not. Pell Grants are awarded to students with exceptional need. You may be eligible for other types of financial aid. The SAR comes in three parts serving different purposes. The student's eligibility status determines which parts of the SAR he or she will receive.

Part 1 - Information Summary

This part serves as an eligibility letter to the student. The EFC is printed on the upper right corner of the first page, under the date. The remainder of the page contains instructions for the student. A summary of the student's information is printed on the back of Part 1 along with certification statements to be signed by the student: the Statement of Updated Information, Statement of Educational Purpose/Certification Statement on Refunds and Default, and Statement of Selective Service Registration Status.

Part 2 - Information Review Form/ Information Request Form

The student uses the Information Review Form to make corrections if necessary. Part 2 has an expanded listing of the student's information under the "You told us" column, with space for the student to correct the information under the column headed "The correct answer is." Data elements that are questioned are highlighted in bold type in Part 2. Part 2 is two pages (four sides) in length if the student is dependent, one page if the student is independent. The Information Request Form, rather than the Review Form, is produced when information provided by the student is rejected. This form provides space for the student to confirm data and provide new data. The Information Request Form must be completed correctly and returned to the FAFSA processor for the student to receive Federal student aid. Corrections to the SAR information may also be made electronically through the EDE system. Check with the school to see if they have the capability to make changes electronically.

Part 3 - Federal Pell Grant Payment Voucher

If the student is eligible for a Federal Pell Grant, the Pell Grant Payment Voucher is added to the Student Aid Report. This signed report is needed for the school to report the Pell Grant payment to the Department's Pell Grant Disbursement System.

Making Corrections on the Student Aid Report

To correct the SAR, the student must enter the correct information for that line item on Part 2 of the SAR, and mail Part 2 back to the FAFSA processor that produced it. The student and spouse must sign Part 2 when submitting corrections; the parents of a dependent student must also sign. The most common changes occur when you estimate your taxes. If you did estimate taxes, the following lines usually will have to be corrected (for both student and parent income):

1. Tax return status – it should have
   changed from estimated to completed.
2. Adjusted Gross Income
3. U.S. taxes paid
4. Income earned from work

Other changes that must be made if incorrect on the SAR are Dependency Status, Number of Family Members and Number of College Students.

If the student wants reports sent to additional schools, he or she may use the SAR correction form to do so. Simply add the new schools to the right of the original schools in "The correct answer is" column and return it to the processor.

Note: A family cannot update asset information to reflect changes to the family's financial situation that took place after the initial application.

When all of the information is completed and correct on the SAR, sign all parts (Parts 1, 2, and 3) and send the originals to the school your child plans to attend. If the student hasn't decided which school he/she plans to attend, most schools will tell you to retain the forms until a final decision is made. If you have questions regarding this area, contact the Financial Aid Officer at the schools you are applying to.

Telephone Numbers

For information on any of the Federal student aid programs the student may call the **Federal Student Aid Information Center**, between the hours of 9:00 a.m. and 5:30 p.m. (Eastern Standard Time), Monday through Friday:

1 (800) 4 FED AID (433-3243)

The Information Center provides the following services at the toll-free number listed above:

☐ Helping you file an application or correct an SAR.

☐ Checking on whether a school takes part in Federal student aid programs.

☐ Explaining student eligibility requirements.

☐ Explaining the process of determining financial aid awards.

☐ Mailing publications.

To find out if your student's application has been processed, or if you want a copy of the Student Aid Report (SAR), call:

INFORMATION CENTER
1 (301) 722-9200

This number is not toll-free, and the Center will not accept collect calls.

"Let me suggest the Aid Package du Jour."

Shopping For Colleges

Why would anyone fish in a stream that has little or no fish in it? If you are looking for financial aid, doesn't it make sense to apply to schools that have excellent aid histories? In addition to looking for the right school to fill the student's academic and personal needs, make aid history another criteria in the selection process. It is no secret that some colleges have more resources than others to spend on their students. Finding this information can be done by researching financial aid publications as well as asking each school the average percent of need they meet. Need is the difference between the total cost of the school and the Expected Family Contribution (EFC). The second criteria to research is the school's percentage of gift aid versus self-help aid (loans and work study).

Statistics, however, can be misleading. XYZ State College has a comprehensive cost of $8,000. XYZ states they meet 99% of demonstrated need. Furthermore, you discover they have no institutional aid to offer. The reason they can meet 99% of need is due to their low cost. There just isn't that much need that can be demonstrated. Federal and State aid programs alone will result in the need being met. The same amount of aid applied to a private school with a cost of $16,000 would leave a huge deficit.

Check the percentage of gift aid that comes directly from the college. Often, a school will advertise that their students received "X" amount of dollars of gift aid. Gift aid includes Federal and State grants and outside scholarships as well as institutional aid. What percent of gift aid is from *institutional sources?*

The most worthless piece of recruiting information I have seen are the schools that tout, "Over 90% (or whatever number) of our students are receiving financial aid." For all you know, 90% of their students could be receiving only a $500 Federal Stafford Loan!

Merit Versus Need

Merit aid is based on a student's academic, athletic and/or extracurricular excellence. Need-based aid is based solely on the family's financial and personal situation.

There are many schools whose only determinant for financial aid is need. There are some schools who offer both need and merit aid.

Rather than writing a philosophical discourse on the attributes or detriments of merit and need-based aid, I prefer to approach both forms of aid from the standpoint of where the student can benefit most.

Case scenario: Sally will graduate in the top 5% of her high school class and has exceptional SAT scores. She is applying to four Ivy League schools. None of these schools offer merit aid. In spite of her academic excellence, there is no merit aid at these schools, therefore her financial aid will be totally need-based. Her parents are disappointed that her hard work has not resulted in scholarships at these schools. There is no need-based aid eligibility.

Comment: First and foremost, Sally's academic achievement resulted in her being accepted at a top quality school. This accomplishment is something to be quite proud of. A financial aid solution for

Sally is to apply to a good independent school that offers merit aid. At any Ivy League, she will be one of many exceptional students. At an independent college she would be strongly recruited and possibly could receive a full scholarship. This approach reverts to the basic concept of supply and demand.

Students who are searching for any form of merit aid should consider the type or class of school where they will be most desirable.

Students searching for need-based aid should be applying to schools with good aid histories. *(Read the previous section: Shopping For Colleges.)*

Evaluating The Award Letter

The financial aid package offered to the student by the college comes in the form of an award letter. Most award letters can be broken down into four components.

1. Estimated Cost of Attendance

2. Family Resources (contribution)

3. Financial Aid Awards

4. Acceptance/ Declination and Signature

1. The cost of attendance *should* include tuition, fees, room and board, books and an allowance for travel and personal expenses. The financial aid administrator at the school the student is attending is responsible for calculating the student's cost based on formulas provided by law. If the total budgeted cost of attendance does not appear on an award letter, the student should request that information when comparing financial aid packages to other schools.

2. Family resources (or family contribution) is the sum of the parent and student contribution. The Federal Methodology (based on the FAFSA) calculates Expected Family Contribution (EFC) for Federal aid. Now we are faced with how the school (based on their own policies) determines what your EFC is.

I recently reviewed five award letters for the same student with five different expected contributions. One school (which I would love to name) had a family contribution *$2,100 higher* than any of the others. That school subtracted the contribution from the cost of attendance and met the remaining need. This gives the illusion of meeting 100% of the student's demonstrated need until you compare it to another school. If this practice was the norm, all that schools would have to do to claim 100% need met would be to increase EFC to the point where they would satisfy the rest.

3. The Financial Aid Award is a listing of the kinds and amounts of aid offered. It will itemize Federal, State and/or Institutional aid. Financial aid includes grants, scholarships, loans and work study programs. The different loans and programs are often confusing if this is the first time you have encountered them. It is always in your best interest to understand what is being offered you.

4. If the student is pleased with his or her aid package, all he or she needs to do is sign it and return it to the respective school. If the student does not want a loan or work study, he or she may decline that part of the award. If the student or parents are dissatisfied with the aid offer, read the next section, "Negotiating Your Aid Package." Since schools are not identically priced, the amount of the aid package is not an accurate measure for comparison. A simple formula that works is as follows:

Add all Stafford and Perkins loans to work study and any grants or scholarships. (Do not include any PLUS loans, or any loans made to the parents.) Subtract the sum from the total cost of the school. (See #1, Cost of Attendance.) Compare this number to other schools' award packages. The school with the lowest number is the school that will cost you the least. You then may want to compare the better packages, noting grants or scholarships. Incidentally, in most cases a PLUS loan is available to the parents regardless of whether or not it is included in the award letter.

To illustrate how award letters may vary, observe the following:

SAMPLE AWARD LETTERS

	SCHOOL A	SCHOOL B	SCHOOL C
TOTAL COST:	$16,500	$18,000	$24,000
Parent Contribution	7,000	7,400	8,500
Student Contribution	1,200	1,000	1,500
Family Contribution	$ 8,200	$ 8,400	$10,000
Financial Need	$ 8,300	$ 9,600	$14,000
FINANCIAL AID:			
College Grant	$ 2,000	$ 500	$ 8,000
Stafford Loan	2,625	2,625	2,625
Work Study	1,200	800	1,400
Perkins Loan	800	1,000	1,200
State Aid	775	775	775
Total Award	$7,400	$5,700	$14,000

School A will cost the family $9,100 ($16,500 - $7,400), School B $12,300 and School C $10,000.

Negotiating Your Aid Package

Before discussing how to negotiate an aid package, it is important to understand why some colleges are not meeting a student's financial need. As stated previously, many schools do not have the resources other schools have. Since financial aid departments often have a fixed amount of money to disburse, they have to appropriate those funds to as many needy students as possible. Inevitably, these monies will run out. Also, (in defense of financial aid officers) recruiters, coaches and admissions staff often boast to prospective parents and students about how much money the school has, thus conveying a false sense of security that the financial aid department has unlimited funds. Finally, with Federal and state cutbacks, colleges are either forced to dig deeper into their own pockets to meet need or they are coming up short. We may see a time when the best package isn't from the school that meets 100% of need, but from the school with the smallest aid gap.

The first principle to keep in mind is that the financial aid package awarded to an incoming freshman will most likely be his or her best package. Barring any major change in the family's financial or personal situation, the student's first year award is critical. The primary reason for this is recruitment. The college will do everything possible to attract a good student to their school. Once the student is enrolled, the student will most likely return the following year. I am not suggesting that in subsequent years, schools drastically cut financial aid; if this was policy, there would be serious retention problems.

Asking a financial aid officer to reevaluate an aid package is not inappropriate. Private schools are more likely to adjust their aid packages than state-supported schools. Unfortunately, shopping the best aid package at some schools is not unlike buying a new car. If you're content with paying sticker price, you will often pay more than the next buyer. I can recall no less than six situations this past year where parents have told me that a certain college would, at minimum, match any other school's award package. There are schools that consistently send poor award letters out the first time and then adjust packages for the students or parents who complain. I call this the "Oil The Squeakiest Wheel Syndrome." Unfortunately, many people are uncomfortable or embarrassed to ask for more. Keep in mind that the worst a school can do is keep your package as it is.

Most colleges will attempt to offer a reasonable award letter the first time around. If you believe that your aid is lacking, call or write the financial aid officer who prepared your package. Explain the part of your family situation that isn't covered on the financial aid form. Be able to document and substantiate what you tell them. Make them aware if another school has offered a better package. They should also know that their school is the student's first, but not only, choice. Do not substitute a PLUS loan for need-based aid when negotiating or comparing aid packages.

Finally, if a school doesn't have the resources or desire to give you the financial aid that you believe you're entitled to, move on to another school. Don't be surprised if you get a call in the Spring with a better offer.

Verification

Verification is the process of checking the accuracy of the information entered on the financial aid form. Not all students go through this process and it isn't (or at least shouldn't be) a traumatic experience. Verification is only required for certain applicants, but the financial aid department may elect to verify the application information of any student who applies for Federal student aid. If submitted information falls out of certain norms or shows inconsistencies, your likelihood for verification increases.

The most common items verified include untaxed income benefits, total income, number of family members in your household, number of family members attending college at least half-time, and assets.

If you show considerable unearned income (interest and dividends) on your tax return, and don't have a comparable amount of assets listed on the financial aid form, a red flag may be raised. For example:

Mr. Jones had $1,800 interest earnings on his tax return. He listed $3,500 of savings on his child's financial aid form. It doesn't take a rocket scientist to figure out that a lot more than $3,500 in savings would be needed to generate $1,800 of interest. If you divide $1,800 by 5 percent (an average rate today), you would arrive at $36,000. That is the amount of principle needed to generate $1,800 of interest. The same principle will apply to dividends, capital gains and any other income that shows up on a tax return. Perhaps the money was spent for a new car or as a downpayment for a new home. As long as you can explain the discrepancy, there should be no problem.

Many colleges will ask for copies of tax returns and W-2s for routine verification checks. If a tax return has not yet been filed and a filing extension was granted, they may accept copies of Form W-2 and a copy of Form 4868, "Application for Automatic Extension of Time to File U.S. Individual Income Tax Return."

I often tell my clients that half of their life story is evident by looking at their tax return and about 75% of their life story by looking at a completed Federal financial aid form. There are tracks and trails everywhere on the form. Tell the truth— it's the law. If you effectively plan for college aid, you will never have anything to hide and you will maximize your aid eligibility.

"Do you have any babysitting money stashed away?"

SAMPLE FINANCIAL AID PACKAGE
$9,000 NEED

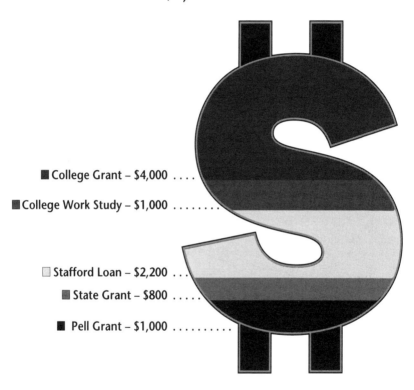

■ College Grant – $4,000 . . . .

■ College Work Study – $1,000 . . . .

▢ Stafford Loan – $2,200 . . .

■ State Grant – $800 . . . . .

■ Pell Grant – $1,000 . . . .

FEDERAL AID PROGRAMS

The Federal Stafford Loan (FSL)

Federal Stafford Loans are low-interest loans to students attending school at least half-time. To be eligible for a subsidized Stafford, the student must demonstrate need.

The current borrowing limits on these loans are:

$2,625 per year for first year undergraduates enrolled in a program of study that is a full academic year.

$3,500 if the student completed the first full year of study and the remainder of his/her program is a full academic year.

$5,500 per year if the student completed two years of study and the remainder of his/her program is at least one academic year.

For periods of undergraduate study that are less than an academic year, the amounts which can be borrowed will be less than those stated. The school's financial aid officer can provide those limits.

Federal Stafford Loans are not made to under-graduates enrolled less than 1/3 of an academic year.

Graduate students can borrow up to $8,500 per year.

The student cannot borrow more than the cost of education at his/her school minus any other financial aid received.

The total Federal Stafford Loan debt any undergraduate student may acquire is limited to $23,000; the total debt for any graduate or professional student is $65,500, including any Federal Stafford Loans received as an undergraduate.

Subsidized versus Unsubsidized

With a need-based Federal Stafford Loan, the Federal government pays the interest on the loan while the student is in school or in deferment. This type of loan is called a "subsidized" Stafford Loan. With a non-need-based Stafford Loan, the student is responsible for the interest during in-school and deferment periods. This is an "unsubsidized" Federal Stafford Loan. The lender holding the loan may let the interest accumulate until the student is out of school or until deferment ends. This will, however, increase the amount of the loan principal.

Now it is possible for students to obtain a Stafford Loan regardless of financial need. It is also possible to have a "combination" loan, based partly on need and partly not on need, as long as the borrowing limits are not exceeded.

Applying for the Stafford Loan

Stafford Loans are made by a lender, such as a bank, credit union or savings and loan institution, but the school itself may also act as the lender. These loans are insured by the guaranty agency in each state and reinsured by the Federal government.

To apply, obtain an application from the lender, complete the student section, and send the application to the school the student plans to attend. The school must complete its part, certifying enrollment, cost of education and any other financial aid to be received. Financial need is evaluated to determine if the student qualifies for a subsidized Federal Stafford Loan. The school must first determine eligibility for a Federal Pell Grant. If eligible, the amount of the Pell Grant will be considered in determining the financial aid package so the student won't be overawarded.

The school can refuse to certify the loan application, or can certify a loan for an amount less than the student would otherwise be eligible for, if the school documents the reason for its action and notifies the student in writing. The school's decision is final and cannot be appealed to the Department of Education.

Not every lender participates in the Federal Stafford Loan Program, so the family should begin looking for one as soon as the student is accepted by the school. To find out who the lenders are in your state, contact your state's guaranty agency for information about the Federal Stafford Loan Program.

If the student receives a subsidized Stafford Loan, he/she will pay an "origination fee" of 5 percent which will be deducted proportionately from each loan disbursement made. This fee is passed on to the Federal government to help reduce the government's cost for these loans. The lender may also collect an insurance premium of up to 3 percent of the loan principal, which is also deducted proportionately from each disbursement. If the student receives an unsubsidized Stafford Loan, an origination/insurance fee of 6.5 percent will be deducted proportionately from each loan disbursement.

Once the student signs a promissory note agreeing to repay the loan, the loan proceeds are made payable to either the student or to both the student and the school. The school will pay the student directly, credit the student's account, or combine these methods. Payment can be made as often as weekly or monthly, if the lender agrees, and only in equal installments. No payment may exceed one-half of the loan amount.

Loan Repayment

After the student graduates, leaves school, or drops below half-time, the student has a six-month "grace period" before loan repayment on a *subsidized* Stafford Loan must begin. No principal or interest payment is required during that time. If the student has an *unsubsidized* Stafford Loan, he/she is responsible for the interest during the six month period.

Within 120 days after leaving school, the organization holding the loan must notify the student of the date repayment begins. The student, however, is responsible for beginning repayment on time, regardless of this notice.

When the student graduates, leaves school, or drops below half-time, he/she must notify the organization holding the loan. That organization may not be the lender that made the loan, as many lenders sell their loans or use servicing organizations to handle the loan and collections. The student must be given the name of the organization that holds the loan, and must also be notified when the loan is sold, if the sale results in the student making payments to a new organization. The old and new organizations must each notify the student of the sale, the identity of the new organization holding the loan, the name and address of the organization to which the student must make payments, and the telephone numbers of both the old and new organizations.

The amount of each payment depends on the size of the debt and on the length of the repayment period. Usually, the student will pay $50.00 per month. However, if the Stafford Loan was first disbursed on or after July 1, 1993 and the student had no outstanding Stafford Loan on the date the he/she signed the promissory note, the student has a repayment option: No later than six months before the date the first payment is due, the lender must offer the student the option of repaying the loan based on a "graduated" or "income-sensitive" repayment. This means the student's financial situation is taken into account in determining the monthly payment.

The following chart shows estimated monthly payment and total interest charges for 7 percent loans of varying amounts, with typical repayment periods. 9 percent is the highest the interest can be.

TYPICAL REPAYMENT PLANS

TOTAL LOAN AMOUNT	NUMBER OF PAYMENTS	MONTHLY PAYMENT	INTEREST CHARGES	TOTAL REPAID
$2,625	66	$50.00	$ 545	$3,170
5,000	120	58.05	1,966	6,966
7,500	120	87.08	2,950	10,450
10,000	120	116.11	3,933	13,933
15,000	120	174.16	5,899	20,899

Deferment of Federal Stafford Loan

Under certain conditions it is possible to defer (postpone) repayment of a Stafford Loan, as long as it is not in default. Default is the failure to repay a student loan according to the terms agreed to when the student signed a promissory note. Refer to the chart on Page 78 for a list of deferments available if the loan was first disbursed on or after July 1, 1993, and the student had no outstanding Federal Stafford Loan, Federal PLUS loan, Federal Supplemental Loans for Students or consolidation loan on the date the promissory note was signed. For a student not in that category, he/she must check with the organization holding the loan for deferments that apply to that loan.

Deferments are not automatic; the student must request one from the organization that holds the loan, and provide documentation to support the request for deferment.

Principal and interest will be deferred for subsidized Stafford Loans, but the student will be responsible for paying the interest on an unsubsidized Stafford.

If the student is willing, but unable, to meet the repayment schedule and is not eligible for a deferment, he/she may be granted forbearance. "Forbearance" is a period of time during which the student won't have to repay any principal or interest on the loan. The student must apply, in writing, directly to the organization holding the loan.

Under certain conditions, as long as the student is not in default, there may be circumstances where repayment of a Federal Stafford Loan can be cancelled, such as total and permanent disability, or death of the borrower.

Campus-based Federal Aid Programs

Federal Pell Grants

A Federal Pell Grant is a grant awarded to undergraduates, attending school at least half-time, on the basis of financial need. For the Pell Grant Program, an undergraduate is one who has not earned a bachelor's or professional degree.

The Department of Education guarantees that each participating school receives enough money to pay the Pell Grants of its eligible students. To determine eligibility, the Department of Education uses a standard formula, established by Congress, to evaluate the information reported on the financial aid form. The formula produces the Expected Family Contribution number. For the 1993-94 award year, if the EFC is $2,100 or less, the student may receive a Pell Grant, assuming all other eligibility requirements are met.

Unlike loans, grants do not have to be repaid. The maximum award for the 1993-94 award year is $2,300. The amount awarded depends not only on the family's Expected Family Contribution level, but also on the cost of the school, full- or part-time status, and whether the student attends school for a full academic year or less.

The school will inform the student in writing how and when he/she will be paid and how much the award will be. The school will credit the award towards the student's account, pay the student directly, or combine these methods. The school must pay at least once per term.

Federal Supplemental Educational Opportunity Grants (FSEOG)

A Federal Supplemental Educational Opportunity Grant (FSEOG) is for undergraduates with exceptional financial need, with priority given to Pell Grant recipients. Unlike a Pell, however, each participating school receives only a certain amount of money from the Federal government to fund their FSEOG program. When that money is used up, there are no more awards available for that year. There is no guarantee that every eligible student will be able to receive a FSEOG.

A student's FSEOG eligibility is determined by each individual school. The maximum amount of this award is $4,000 annually, and since it is a grant, it does not have to be repaid.

The school will credit the FSEOG to the student's account, pay the student directly, or combine these methods. Schools must pay students at least once per term, unless the total FSEOG award is $500 or less. In that case, the school may pay the student once during the academic year.

Federal Work-Study (FWS)

The Federal Work-Study (FWS) Program provides jobs for undergraduate and graduate students who need financial aid. FWS provides the student the opportunity to earn money to help pay for educational expenses. The program encourages community service work.

The pay for FWS is at least the Federal minimum wage, but it may also be related to the type of work and skills required. Undergraduates are paid by the hour; graduate students may be paid by the hour or may receive a salary. The school pays the student directly at least once a month. The amount earned cannot exceed the total Federal Work Study award.

Federal Work Study programs may be either on or off campus. Off-campus jobs usually involve work that is in the public interest, such as a private or public nonprofit organization, or a local, State, or Federal agency. However, some schools may have agreements with private sector employers for FWS jobs. These jobs must be related to the course of study.

The school sets the student's work schedule. In arranging a job and assigning work hours, the school takes into account the student's class schedule, health and academic progress.

Federal Perkins Loan

A Federal Perkins Loan is a low-interest (5%) loan for both undergraduate and graduate students with exceptional financial need, as determined by the school. Perkins Loans are made directly through the school's financial aid office, with the school acting as the lender. These loans must be repaid.

As with the Federal Supplemental Educational Opportunity Grant (FSEOG), each school receives limited monies from the Federal Government with which to fund these loans. Upon qualification, the undergraduate student may borrow up to $3,000 for each year, with a maximum total debt of $15,000. Graduate students who qualify may borrow up to $5,000 for each year of graduate study, with a maximum total debt of $30,000 (including any Perkins Loans taken as an undergraduate).

After the student signs a promissory note agreeing to repay the loan, the school will either pay the student directly or credit the student's account. The loan is received in two payments during the academic year, unless the total Federal Perkins Loan award for that year is $500 or less. Then the school may pay the loan once during the academic year, if it chooses.

FEDERAL LOANS

	SUBSIDIZED STAFFORD LOAN	UNSUBSIDIZED STAFFORD LOAN	SUPPLEMENTAL LOANS FOR STUDENTS	PARENT LOANS FOR UNDERGRADUATE STUDENTS
Maximum Lifetime Amount	Undergraduate: $23,000 Graduate: $65,500	Undergraduate: $23,000 Graduate: $65,500	Undergraduate: $23,000 Graduate: $73,000	Cannot exceed total cost of education minus any aid received
Maximum Repayment Term	10 years	10 years	10 years	10 years
Interest Rate	Varies annually Capped at 9%	Varies annually Capped at 9%	Varies annually Capped at 11%	Varies annually Capped at 10%
Repayment	Repayment of principal and interest begins 6 months after completion of studies (graduation, withdrawal, or less than halftime attendance)	Repayment of principal and interest can be postponed while student is still in school. If interest is postponed, it will be added to the principal upon completion of studies	Repayment of principal and interest can be postponed while student is still in school, or 60 days after loan is disbursed	Repayment begins within 60 days of disbursement

FEDERAL LOANS

	SUBSIDIZED STAFFORD LOAN	UNSUBSIDIZED STAFFORD LOAN	SUPPLEMENTAL LOANS FOR STUDENTS	PARENT LOANS FOR UNDERGRADUATE STUDENTS
Eligibility	Must demonstrate financial need	Not based on financial need *	Must demonstrate financial need	Not based on financial need
	Undergraduate and graduate students	Undergraduate and graduate students	*Independent under-graduate and graduate students*	Parents of *dependent* undergraduate students
	Full or halftime	Full or halftime	Full or halftime	Full or halftime
		* Must complete a financial aid form to qualify		
Maximum Annual Loan Amounts	Year 1: $2,625 Year 2: 3,500 Year 3: 5,500 Year 4: 5,500 Year 5: 5,500	Year 1: $2,625 Year 2: 3,500 Year 3: 5,500 Year 4: 5,500 Year 5: 5,500	Year 1: $4,000 Year 2: 4,000 Year 3: 5,000 Year 4: 5,000 Year 5: 5,000	Total cost of education minus any aid received
	Graduate: 8,500	Graduate: 8,500	Graduate: 10,000	

The student has a period of time before repayment must begin, called a "grace period." A student attending school at least half-time has a grace period of nine months after he/she graduates, leaves school or drops below half-time. If the student is less than half-time, the grace period may be different, and he/she should consult with the financial aid administrator.

At the end of the grace period, the student may begin repaying the loan. He/she may be allowed up to 10 years to repay.

Remember — The campus-based Federal Aid Programs: FSEOG, Federal Work Study, and Federal Perkins Loan funding is limited. Your child could lose the opportunity to receive aid from these sources if you don't apply early!

LOAN DEFERMENT SUMMARY

DEFERMENT CONDITION	PERKINS	STAFFORD	PLUS	SLS
At least half-time study at a post-secondary school	Yes	Yes	Yes	Yes
Study in an approved fellowship program or in a rehabilitation training program for the disabled	Yes	Yes	Yes	Yes
Unable to find full-time employment	Up to 3 Years	Up to 3 Years	Up to 3 Years	Up to 3 Years
Economic hardship	Yes	Yes	Yes	Yes

In Search
Of More Money

Financing the Non-Need Portion of College Costs

Unless your family has virtually no income and assets, you will be responsible for a portion of the total cost of college. Income and/or assets are considered viable sources of funds. In most instances, the family contribution is the minimum amount of money that will be contributed with out-of-pocket funds. Before you run to the bank, consider the future financial aid and taxation consequences of how you borrow.

Student Savings

If there are any assets in the student's name, they should be expended first. As discussed earlier in this book, having assets in the student's name at time of application will result in a 35% assessment of their total savings and investments. There are situations where it is not possible to shelter student assets. If this is the case, using the student's money first will ensure that their assets won't be reassessed at 35% the following year.

Student and Parental Income

Any monies that can be budgeted from income for college expenses will be money that you won't be borrowing and paying interest on. Make an objective of saving $100, $200, etc. every month, specifically to help offset college costs. Two hundred dollars monthly from earnings will decrease a student or parent's debt load by $9,600 in four years (before interest)!

Parental Savings

Monies that are not sheltered in pension-type funds should be highly liquid and a good source of capital. If possible, maintain an emergency fund (at least six months of fixed expenses) in liquid savings for non-college expenditures.

Parental Investments

If the family owns stocks, bonds, mutual funds, etc., they can be liquidated to offset non-need costs. Keep in mind that if you are going to incur large capital gains at sale (in addition to the income tax liability), your income will increase, thus your contribution level for the following year will increase. The opposite effect occurs when you have a capital loss. Your tax liability decreases and your EFC decreases.

Home Equity

Home equity is an excellent source for college funds. As previously stated, the net value of your home (market value minus your mortgage or equity loan) is not assessed for Federal aid but will most likely be assessed for institutional aid. In most cases, the interest will be tax-deductible, thus giving you an added tax benefit.

Consider home equity more cost-effective than a PLUS Loan. The PLUS loan generally requires interest payments within 60 days after the last disbursement. The interest rate is comparable to home equity loans, but like any other consumer loan, the interest is not tax deductible. Furthermore, consumer debt, unlike a home equity loan, does not decrease your net worth for financial aid purposes.

Installment Plans

Many colleges permit tuition payments over 12 months rather than at the beginning of each semester to help families spread out their payments. Some schools will charge no interest on these plans or just a nominal fee at the beginning of the plan. Check with your college to see what type of extended payment plans are offered and look closely at the terms.

PLUS and SLS Loans

PLUS loans are for parents who want to borrow to help pay for their children's education; Supplemental Loans for Students (SLS) are for student borrowers. Both loans provide additional funds for educational expenses and, like Stafford Loans, are made by a lender such as a bank, credit union, or savings and loan association.

PLUS and SLS loans have variable interest rates. These rates are set each June. The interest rate for each loan is shown on the promissory note, signed by the borrower when the loan is made.

The new Federal PLUS Loans enable parents to borrow up to the cost of education minus any financial aid received. Although the loan amounts are attractive, I would suggest parents consider large PLUS loans carefully. These loans can accumulate a very large and possibly insurmountable debt.

Under SLS, graduate students and *independent* undergraduates who are enrolled in a program whose length is a full academic year may borrow up to $4,000 a year for the first two years of undergraduate school and then up to $5,000 a year for year 3-5. The maximum loan for a graduate student is $10,000 a year. This amount is in addition to the Stafford Loan limits. (In exceptional circumstances, the financial aid administrator may authorize dependent undergraduates to apply for an SLS.)

Repayment of principal and interest can be postponed while the student is still in school, or payment can begin within 60 days after the loan is disbursed.

Scholarship Search Services

With all the expenses associated with college, mail scholarship search services is one to avoid. Don't be lured by advertising like "Guaranteed Available Sources." All that means is they will provide a list of scholarships or financial aid sources that you could be eligible for. You probably have already applied to many of the sources listed simply by completing your financial aid form. If you are a left-handed Martian, you may be eligible for the other scholarships. The attainable private scholarships can be easily found via the high school guidance office or from the admissions or financial aid office at the college your child is attending. You may also inquire whether your employer offers scholarships for their employees' dependent children. To paraphrase a financial aid officer, "In the last twelve years, I have not seen one student receive a grant or scholarship obtained through a scholarship search service."

*"Have **I** got a deal for **You**!"*

The College Financial Aid Consultant

A relatively new and specialized area of financial planning are planners who help families through the financial aid process. There has been some controversy regarding the practices of financial aid consultants, particularly from the colleges. First and foremost, financial aid consultants are not scholarship search services. In my opinion, the bad press these services receive is well-deserved. The need and importance for a legitimate and competent financial aid specialist can be demonstrated by the term I call, "financial aid perspective." Case in point: Mrs. Brown, the financial aid administrator at a local independent college, has a reputation for doing everything possible to help the students attend her school. Unfortunately, she does not have an unlimited budget and must stretch the grant money out as far as possible. Although Mrs. Brown's sincerity is beyond reproach, there are two inherent perspective problems. First and foremost, Mrs. Brown is employed by the college, not the student. Within her means, she will be accommodating, but her means may be limited and she may be dealing with thousands of students. Second, despite Mrs. Brown's dedication, will she suggest applying to other schools? Will she explain techniques of negotiating a financial aid package, or will she offer suggestions to help increase your financial aid eligibility, knowing that her school doesn't have the means to meet the student's increased need?

A financial aid consultant works for you. He or she has no vested interest in any particular school, governmental agency or lending institution. The consultant is employed to help the family receive the best financial aid package legally possible and has only one vested interest – the client. The end result can be hundreds or thousands of dollars in increased aid eligibility. This is accomplished by having a thorough understanding of the financial aid process and employing sound college financial aid planning principles. This is analogous to tax-accountants suggesting tax reduction strategies to their clients. They are neither unethical or immoral, they are informed. Knowledge is power. With the college costs families are faced with today, you need all you can get.

Author's Choice of Best Schools for Financial Aid

The following colleges and universities have been selected to the Author's "Best Schools For Financial Aid" list. Criterion used includes average percent of need met for incoming freshmen, average percent of need met for upperclassmen, and the percent of gift aid awarded. Information was gathered by questionnaires sent to each school's financial aid administrator, research and/or specific case experience.

Alabama
Birmingham-Southern College — Birmingham

California
California Institute of Technology — Pasadena
Chapman University — Orange
Claremont McKenna College — Claremont
Harvey Mudd College — Claremont
Mills College — Oakland
Occidental College — Los Angeles
Pitzer College — Claremont
Pomona College — Claremont
Scripps College — Claremont
Stanford University — Stanford
Thomas Aquinas College — Santa Paula
University of California, Los Angeles — Los Angeles

Colorado
University of Denver — Denver

Connecticut
Central Connecticut State University — New Britain
Connecticut College — New London
Wesleyan University — Middletown
Yale University — New Haven

District of Columbia
Georgetown University — Washington, D.C.

Georgia
Emory University — Atlanta

Illinois

Augustana College	Rock Island
Blackburn College	Carlinville
College of St. Francis	Joliet
Knox College	Galesburg
Lake Forest College	Lake Forest
Northwestern University	Evanston
Wheaton College	Wheaton

Indiana

DePauw University	Greencastle
Earlham College	Richmond
Hanover College	Hanover
Saint Meinrad College	Saint Meinrad
Taylor University	Upland
Wabash College	Crawfordsville

Iowa

Clarke College	Dubuque
Cornell College	Mount Vernon
Grinnell College	Grinnell
Iowa Wesleyan College	Mount Pleasant
Loras College	Dubuque
University of Dubuque	Dubuque

Maine

Bates College	Lewiston
Bowdoin College	Brunswick
Colby College	Waterville

Maryland

College of Notre Dame of Maryland	Baltimore
Hood College	Federick
Johns Hopkins University	Baltimore
Washington College	Chestertown

Massachusetts

Amherst College	Amherst
Boston University	Boston
Brandeis University	Waltham
College of The Holy Cross	Worcester
Harvard University	Cambridge
Smith College	Northampton
Tufts University	Medford
Wellesley College	Wellesley
Williams College	Williamstown

Michigan
Albion College	Albion
Grand Valley State University	Allendale

Minnesota
Carleton College	Northfield
Concordia College	Moorhead
St. Olaf College	Northfield

New Jersey
Princeton University	Princeton

New York
Alfred University	Alfred
Barnard College	New York
Colgate University	Hamilton
Columbia University, School of Engineering and Applied Science	New York
Cornell University	Ithaca
Hamilton College	Clinton
Jewish Theological Seminary of America	New York
Nazareth College of Rochester	Rochester
Rensselaer Polytechnic Institute	Troy
Sarah Lawrence College	Bronxville
State University of New York at Brockport	Brockport
Union College	Schenectady
University of Rochester	Rochester
Vassar College	Poughkeepsie

North Carolina
Davidson College	Davidson
Duke University	Durham
Meredith College	Raleigh
Wake Forest University	Winston-Salem

Ohio
Antioch College	Yellow Springs
Baldwin-Wallace College	Berea
Case Western Reserve University	Cleveland
College of Wooster	Wooster
Denison University	Granville
Oberlin College	Oberlin
Ohio Wesleyan University	Delaware

Oregon
Reed College	Portland

Pennsylvania

Allegheny College	Meadville
Bryn Mawr College	Bryn Mawr
Carnegie Mellon University	Pittsburgh
Franklin and Marshall College	Lancaster
Gettysburg College	Gettysburg
Haverford College	Haverford
Juniata College	Huntingdon
Lafayette College	Easton
Lehigh University	Bethlehem
St. Charles Borromeo Seminary	Overbrook
Swarthmore College	Swarthmore
Westminster College	New Wilmington

Rhode Island

Brown University	Providence
Rhode Island College	Providence

South Carolina

Converse College	Spartanburg

Tennessee

Rhodes College	Memphis
University of The South	Sewanee

Texas

Rice University	Houston
Trinity University	San Antonio

Vermont

Bennington College	Bennington
Trinity College of Vermont	Burlington

Virginia

Hampden-Sydney College	Hampden-Sydney
Marymount University	Arlington
Roanoke College	Salem
Sweet Briar College	Sweet Briar
University of Richmond	Richmond
Washington and Lee University	Lexington

Wisconsin

Beloit College	Beloit
Lawrence University	Appleton
Ripon College	Ripon
St. Norbert College	De Pere

STATE AGENCIES

Alabama Commission on Higher Education
One Court Square, Suite 221
Montgomery, Alabama 36104
(205) 269-2700

Alaska Commission on Postsecondary Education
P.O. Box FP
Juneau, Alaska 99811
(907) 465-2854

Arizona Commission for Postsecondary Education
2020 North Central Avenue, Suite 1407
Phoenix, Arizona 85012
(602) 229-2593

Arkansas Department of Higher Education
114 East Capitol Street
Little Rock, Arkansas 72201
(501) 324-9300

California Student Aid Commission
P.O. Box 510845
Sacramento, California 94245
(916) 322-9267

Colorado Commission on Higher Education
1300 Broadway, 2nd Floor
Denver, Colorado 80203
(303) 866-2723

Connecticut Board of Higher Education
61 Woodland Street
Hartford, Connecticut 06105
(203) 566-2618

Delaware Postsecondary
  Education Commission
820 North French Street, 4th Floor
Wilmington, Delaware 19801
(302) 577-3240

Department of Human Services
Office of Postsecondary Education,
Research and Assistance
2100 Martin Luther King, Jr. Avenue, SE
Washington, DC 20020
(202) 727-3685

Florida Department of Education
Office of Student Financial Assistance
1344 Florida Education Center
Tallahassee, Florida 32399
(904) 488-1034

Georgia Student Finance Authority
State Loans and Grants Division
2082 East Exchange Place, Suite 200
Tucker, Georgia 30084
(404) 493-5452

Hawaii State Postsecondary
  Education Commission
2444 Dole Street, Room 209
Honolulu, Hawaii 96822
(808) 956-8213

Idaho Office of the State Board of Education
650 West State Street, Room 307
Boise, Idaho 83720
(208) 334-2270

Illinois State Student Assistance Commission
106 Wilmot Road
Deerfield, Illinois 60015
(708) 948-8500

State Student Assistance Commission of Indiana
150 West Market Street, Suite 500
Indianapolis, Indiana 46204
(317) 232-2350

Iowa College Aid Commission
201 Jewitt Building
Ninth and Grand Avenue
Des Moines, Iowa 50309
(515) 281-3501

Kansas Board of Regents
400 South West 8th Street, Suite 609
Topeka, Kansas 66603
(913) 296-3517

Kentucky Higher Education Assistance Authority
1050 U.S. 127 South, Suite 102
Frankfort, Kentucky 40601
(502) 564-4928

Louisiana Student Financial Assistance Commission
P.O. Box 91202
Baton Rouge, Louisiana 70821
(504) 922-1150

Finance Authority of Maine
83 Western Avenue
P.O. Box 949
Augusta, Maine 04333
(207) 289-2183

Maryland State
  Scholarship Administration
16 Francis Street
Annapolis, Maryland 21401
(410) 974-5370

Massachusetts Board of
  Regents of Higher Education
Scholarship Office
330 Stuart Street
Boston, Massachusetts 02116
(617) 727-9420

Michigan Department of Education
Scholar and Tuition Grant Program
P.O. Box 30008
Lansing, Michigan 48909
(517) 373-3394

Minnesota Higher Education Coordinating Board
550 Cedar Street, Suite 400
St. Paul, Minnesota 55101
(612) 296-9657

Mississippi Postsecondary Education
  Financial Assistance Board
3825 Ridgewood Road
Jackson, Mississippi 39211
(601) 982-6570

Missouri Coordinating Board
  for Higher Education
101 Adams Street
Jefferson City, Missouri 65101
(314) 751-2361

Montana University System
2500 Broadway
Helena, Montana 59620
(406) 444-6594

Nebraska Coordinating Commission
  for Postsecondary Education
301 Centennial Mall South
P.O. Box 95005
Lincoln, Nebraska 68509
(402) 471-2847

Nevada State Department of Education
Capitol Complex
400 West King Street
Carson City, Nevada 89710
(702) 687-5915

New Hampshire Postsecondary
  Education Commission
2 Industrial Park Drive
Concord, New Hampshire 03301
(603) 271-2555

New Jersey Department of Higher Education
Office of Grants and Scholarships
4 Quakerbridge Plaza CN 540
Trenton, New Jersey 08625
(609) 588-3268

New Mexico Commission on Higher Education
1068 Cerrillos Road
Santa Fe, New Mexico 87501
(505) 827-7383

New York State
  Higher Education Services Corporation
One Commerce Plaza
Albany, New York 12255
(518) 473-0431

North Carolina State
  Education Assistance Authority
P.O. Box 2688
Chapel Hill, North Carolina 27515
(919) 549-8614

North Dakota State Board
  of Higher Education
Student Financial Assistance Program
600 East Boulevard
Bismarck, North Dakota 58505
(701) 224-4114

Ohio Board of Regents
Student Assistance Office
3600 State Office Tower
30 East Broad Street
Columbus, Ohio 43266
(614) 466-1191

Oklahoma Tuition Aid Grant Program
P.O. Box 3020
Oklahoma City, Oklahoma 73101
(405) 552-4356

Oregon State Scholarship Commission
1445 Willamette Street
Eugene, Oregon 97401
(503) 346-4166

Pennsylvania
 Higher Education Assistance Agency
660 Boas Street
Harrisburg, Pennsylvania 17102
(717) 257-2800

Rhode Island Higher Education
 Assistance Authority
560 Jefferson Boulevard
Warwick, Rhode Island 02886
(401) 277-2050

South Carolina Higher Education
 Tuition Grants Commission
P.O. Box 12159
Columbia, South Carolina 29211
(803) 734-1200

South Dakota Department of
 Education and Cultural Affairs
Office of the Secretary
700 Governors Drive
Pierre, South Dakota 57501
(605) 773-3134

Tennessee Student
 Assistance Corporation
404 James Robertson Parkway, Suite 1950
Nashville, Tennessee 37243
(615) 741-1346

Texas Higher Education Coordinating Board
7745 Chevy Chase Drive, Buildings 4 & 5
Austin, Texas 78752
(512) 483-6340

Utah System of Higher Education
355 West North Temple
#3 Triad Center, Suite 550
Salt Lake City, Utah 84180
(801) 538-5247

Vermont Student Assistance Corporation
Champlain Mill
P.O. Box 2000
Winooski, Vermont 05404
(802) 655-9602

State Council of Higher Education for Virginia
101 North Fourteenth Street
Richmond, Virginia 23219
(804) 225-2623

Washington State Higher Education Coordinating Board
917 Lakeridge Morris Business Park
Mail Stop GV-11
Olympia, Washington 98504
(206) 586-6404

Central Office of the State College and University
  Systems of West Virginia
P.O. Box 4007
Charleston, West Virginia 25364
(304) 347-1211

Wisconsin Higher Educational Aids Board
131 West Wilson Street, Suite 902
P.O. Box 7885
Madison, Wisconsin 53707
(608) 266-1660

Wyoming Community College Commission
Herschler Building 1W
122 West 25th Street
Cheyenne, Wyoming 82002
(307) 777-7763

GLOSSARY

Adjusted Gross Income: The sum of earned income, unearned income, and business income, less adjustments to income.

American College Testing Program (ACT): One of several contracted needs analysis processing centers; located in Iowa City, Iowa.

Award Letter: Letter notifying the student of the type of financial aid package the school is offering for the school year.

Award Year: The award year, for financial aid purposes, is from July 1st to June 30th.

Citizen/Eligible Noncitizen: To receive Federal student aid, a student must be either a U.S. citizen, a U.S. national (includes natives of American Samoa or Swain's Island), or a U.S. permanent resident who has an I-151, I-551, or I-551C Alien Registration Receipt Card

College Scholarship Services (CSS): One of several contracted needs analysis processing centers; located in Princeton, New Jersey.

Consolidation Loan: A loan made when an eligible lender pays off a student's existing student loans and creates one new loan. To be eligible, the existing loans must total at least $7,500 and the student must be in the process of repaying his/her loans (or have entered a grace period).

Cost of Education (or Cost of Attendance): The total amount it will cost a student to go to school, usually expressed as a yearly figure. The cost of education covers tuition and fees, on-campus room and board (or a housing and food allowance for off-campus students), and allowances for books, supplies, transportation, child care, costs related to a disability, and miscellaneous expenses.

Deadline: The date by which each individual school requires the FAFSA and FAF be completed and received by the processing center. The forms cannot be mailed out until after January 1; most schools set deadlines early in the calendar year. If applying to schools with different deadlines, the forms must be mailed out prior to the earliest required date.

Default: Failure to repay a student loan according to the terms agreed to when the student signed a promissory note. Default also may result from failure to submit a request for deferment or cancellation on time.

Dependent Student: A student who, for financial aid purposes, is classified as dependent on his/her parents for his/her primary support; when applying for financial aid, the parents' income and asset information will be reported along with the dependent student's.

Dislocated Worker: A person certified as such by a state agency, such as a state employment service or job service. Generally, a dislocated worker is someone who meets at least one of the following conditions:

- has been terminated or laid off, or has received notice of termination or layoff,

- has been terminated or has received notice of termination from a plant or other facility that has permanently closed,

- has been unemployed for a long period and has limited opportunity for reemployment in the same or similar occupation in the area where the person resides,

- was self-employed (including farmers) but is now unemployed because of poor economic conditions in the community or because a natural disaster has occurred.

If the student, student's spouse, or - if dependent - one of the student's parents, is certified as a dislocated worker because of one of the above conditions, the family's financial circumstances will be specially considered in determining the ability to pay for the student's education.

Educational Asset Protection Allowance: The amount of assets that are not included as available assets in the Federal Methodology.

Expected Family Contribution: An amount, determined by a formula established by Congress, that indicates how much of the family's financial resources should be available to help pay college costs.

Federal Aid: Student financial aid programs sponsored by the U.S. Department of Education. Includes Federal Pell Grants, Federal Supplemental Educational Opportunity Grants (FSEOG), Federal Work-Study (FWS), Federal Perkins Loans, Federal Stafford Loans, Federal PLUS Loans, and Federal Supplemental Loans For Students (SLS).

Federal Needs Analysis Methodology: The formula, established by Congress, that calculates the student's Expected Family Contribution level.

Federal Pell Grant: A grant awarded to undergraduates attending school at least half-time, on the basis of financial need.

Federal Perkins Loan: A low-interest loan (5%) for undergraduate and graduate students with exceptional financial need, as determined by the school.

Federal PLUS Loan: A loan for parents which enable them to borrow for each child who is enrolled at least half-time and is a dependent student. The annual loan limit is the student's cost of education minus any financial aid received.

Federal Stafford Loan: Low-interest loan made to undergraduate and graduate students attending school at least half-time.

Federal Supplemental Education Opportunity Grant (FSEOG): A grant awarded to undergraduates with exceptional financial need, as determined by the school, with priority given to Federal Pell Grant recipients.

Federal Supplemental Loans for Students: Loans available to independent undergraduate, graduate or professional students, enrolled at least half-time. The annual loan limit is the student's cost of education minus any other financial aid received.

Federal Unsubsidized Stafford Loan: Low-interest loan made to undergraduate and graduate students attending school at least half-time. Interest is paid by the student rather than subsidized by the Federal government.

Federal Work-Study (FWS): A program which provides jobs for undergraduate and graduate students who need financial aid. FWS provides the student the opportunity to earn money to help pay for educational expenses.

Financial Aid Administrator: A person employed by the college or university who is responsible for the administration and distribution of financial aid to its students.

Financial Aid Form (FAF): Used in conjunction with the FAFSA, the FAF further qualifies the student for institutional and/or state aid. This application requires a processing fee.

Financial Aid Package: The total financial aid a student receives. Federal, state, and institutional aid, such as grants, loans, or work-study, are combined in a "package" to help meet the student's financial need.

Financial Need: The difference between the student's cost of attendance and the Expected Family Contribution.

Forbearance: A period of time during which a student will not have to repay any principal or interest on a Federal Stafford Loan, if that student is willing, but unable, to meet the repayment schedule.

Free Application for Federal Student Aid (FAFSA): The application filled out by the student that collects household and financial information to be used to calculate the Expected Family Contribution. This application qualifies the student for Federal aid programs.

Gift Aid: Type of financial aid which the student does not have to repay; includes grants and scholarships.

Grace Period: The period of time before repayment of a student loan must begin. Depending on the type of loan, the student will have a grace period of six to nine months after he/she graduates, leaves school or drops below half-time.

Grant: Federal, state and/or institutional financial aid which the student does not have to repay; "gift aid."

Guaranty Agency: The organization that administers the Federal Stafford Loan, Federal PLUS, and Federal SLS programs in each state. The Federal Government sets loan limits and interest rates, but each state is free to set its own additional limitations, within Federal guidelines.

Half-Time: At schools measuring progress by credit hours and academic terms (semesters, trimester, or quarters), "half-time" means at least 6 semester hours or quarter hours per term. At schools measuring progress by credit hours but not using academic terms, "half-time" means at least 12 semester hours or 18 quarter hours per year. Individual schools may choose to set higher minimums than these. Federal Stafford Loan, Federal PLUS, and Federal SLS requirements may also be slightly different.

Higher Education Amendments of 1992: The changes made to the financial aid programs by the Department of Education as a result of reauthorization.

Independent Student: A student who, for financial aid purposes, is classified as not having access to parental support and may exclude parent's income and assets when completing the financial aid forms. The criteria for determining independence for Federal, state and institutional aid may differ.

Institutional Aid: Student financial aid disseminated by the schools, usually in the form of grants and need-based scholarships.

Legal Guardian: An individual appointed by the courts to provide support for the student.

Merit Aid: Financial aid awarded on the basis of the student's academic, athletic, and/or extracurricular excellence.

Need Analysis: The process of analyzing the household and financial information on the student's financial aid application and calculating an Expected Family Contribution.

Need-Based Aid: Financial aid awarded on the basis of the family's financial and personal situation.

Needs Analysis Processing Center: An agency contracted by the Department of Education to process completed financial aid forms.

Origination Fee: A fee deducted from each disbursement of a Federal loan for processing and insurance costs.

Preparer: An individual, other than the student, student's spouse, or student's parent, who completes the Free Application for Federal Student Aid. The law requires that such an individual complete and sign the Preparer section of the FAFSA, even if he/she is not paid for his/her services.

Professional Judgement: The ability of the Financial Aid Administrator to make adjustments in the Formula used to calculate the Expected Family Contribution due to "special conditions," for example, excessive medical expenses, or to override a student's dependency status. Adjustments are made on a case-by-case basis.

Promissory Note: The binding legal documents signed when the student gets a student loan. It lists the conditions under which the student is borrowing and the terms of repayment. It also includes information regarding the interest, deferment, and cancellation provisions.

Self-Help: Type of financial aid which the student must either repay or work for (loans and work-study).

Special Conditions: Special circumstances, such as excessive medical expenses, elementary or secondary private school tuition, loss of job, death, or divorce, which would impact the parent's ability to pay college costs. In such a situation, the Financial Aid Administrator may use "professional judgement" to adjust the Expected Family Contribution.

Student Aid Report (SAR): The document printed by the needs-analysis processing center which contains the financial and other information reported on the Free Application for Federal Student Aid. This report is mailed to the student approximately four weeks after submission of the FAFSA, and indicates the student's Expected Family Contribution level.

Unearned Income: Will include interest, dividends and capital gains.

Untaxed Income: Income which must be reported on the financial aid forms and includes deductible IRA's, Keogh's, tax-sheltered annuities, 401k plans, workers compensation, earned income credits, and certain welfare benefits.

Verification: The process of checking the accuracy of the information entered on the financial aid form. Verification is performed by the college that the student is or will be attending.